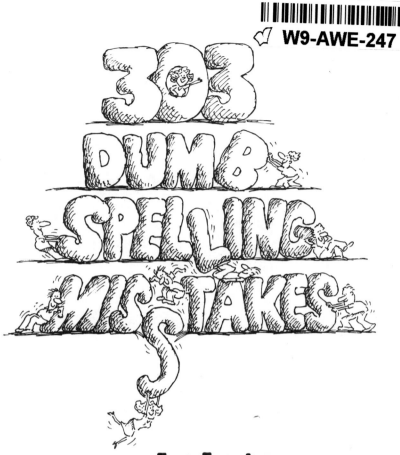

...and what you can do about them

David Downing
Elizabethtown College

Illustrations by Mario Risso

National Textbook Company
a division of NTC/CONTEMPORARY PUBLISHING GROUP
Lincolnwood, Illinois USA

ISBN: 0-8442-5475-4

Published by National Textbook Company,
a division of NTC/Contemporary Publishing Group, Inc.,
4255 West Touhy Avenue,
Lincolnwood (Chicago), Illinois 60646-1975 U.S.A.
©1990 by NTC/Contemporary Publishing Group, Inc.
Manufactured in the United States of America.

8 9 VP 9 8 7 6

Introduction

Absence makes the heart grow fonder. Or is it *absense*? Words like these separate good spellers from bad spellers. Or is it *seperate*? If you can't remember how to spell *absence* or *separate*, don't feel bad. You're not alone.

A great many words in American English deserve to be misspelled. We often spell *glamour* with a *u*, like the British, but we leave this *u* out of *glamorous.* The word *through* doesn't rhyme with *bough, cough, dough,* or *rough,* but it does rhyme with *to, two,* and *too.*

The dramatist George Bernard Shaw illustrated just how ludicrous spelling can become when he pointed out that the word *fish* can quite logically be spelled *ghoti: gh* as in *laugh*, *o* as in *women,* and *ti* as in *nation.*

If you're not thoroughly confused by now, you're not paying attention. In Spanish or German, words are generally spelled just as they sound. In English, one's only hope is a good memory. Some of America's most celebrated thinkers and writers have been notoriously bad spellers. F. Scott Fitzgerald, one of America's most distinguished novelists, was an atrocious speller. He used to address letters to his good friend "Earnest Hemmingway" misspelling both the first and last names of Ernest Hemingway.

The only spelling rule in English that is worth much is this:

> *i* before *e*
> except after *c*
> or when sounded like *ay*
> as in *neighbor* and *weigh*

That's well and good for *receive, deceive,* and their cousins, as well as for *neighbor* and *weigh.* But what about *weird* and *sovereign* and *counterfeit* and more than thirty other exceptions? What rule tells us when the rules apply and when they don't?

Spelling in English is not a matter of logic, sounding out words, or learning rules. It is simply a matter of remembering how a word looks on the page. Some people remember spelling without trying, just as some people remember phone numbers without trying. Most of us, however, have to rely on phone books and dictionaries.

Keep in mind that some phone numbers are easier to remember than others. You would want to write down *960-3182,* but you might not need a pencil if the number were *123-4567.* Likewise, a number is easy to recall if it spells out a word on the phone dial. Could you remember the number of a jeweler if I told you to call 1(800) 289-4367? How about if I gave it to you as 1(800) BUY-GEMS?

Like remembering phone numbers, good spelling is based on two principles:

PRINCIPLE NUMBER ONE: A pattern is easier to remember than a random assortment.

Below are two sets of 25 letters.

COLUMN A	COLUMN B
seven	fyquv
shorn	pxlza
sheep	rsdwt
stood	mydkj
still	cbguh

Which column would you prefer to memorize? Column A, of

course. It can be memorized in an instant. On the other hand, the letters in Column B would take a few minutes to learn, and even then you are likely to make mistakes. That's because the first column is full of patterns; the letters make up words, the words make up a sentence, and they all start with *s.* In the second column, however, you have to rely on painstaking memorization of individual letters.

PRINCIPLE NUMBER TWO: It is easier to remember something if you can visualize it.

People often say, "I can't recall the name, but I never forget a face." And it's true. Our imaginations can store mental pictures much more effectively and permanently than our intellects can store individual bits of information. If I asked you, "Who was our twenty-sixth President?" you probably couldn't answer, even if you have seen a list of U.S. Presidents sometime recently. But if I showed you his picture, chances are you'd recognize him at once as Theodore Roosevelt.

The secret of good spelling is to invent patterns and pictures to help you recall the hard parts of hard words. Rather than memorizing spelling rules or spelling lists, or trying to sound out difficult words, try enlisting the aid of your visual imagination.

When you come across a word you are likely to misspell, focus on the part of the word that gives you the most trouble. It may be an unaccented vowel. (Is it *correspondance* or *correspondence*?) Or it may be a question of doubling consonants (*satellite, sattelite,* or *satelite*?).

In the first example above, the correct spelling is *correspondence with an e.* You can remember the e by thinking of your correspond**en**ce going into an **en**velope. In the second example, it's one *t* and two *l*'s. Notice the word *tell* in the middle of sa**tell**ite. If you remember that satellites **tell** us more about our world, you will also remember how to spell the word correctly.

In my years of college teaching, I have corrected at least 50,000 misspellings. That number would be staggering if I had actually circled that many *different* misspelled words. But I haven't run across 50,000 misspelled words, or even

5,000. Rather, it is the same three or four hundred words that I see misspelled over and over and over again.

This book is a collection of some of those commonly misspelled words, along with mnemonic patterns and pictures. Some of these memory devices are logical and some are not. Some are humorous and some are not. But all of them should help you lock the correct spelling into your visual memory. I've had students laugh or groan when I drew one of these on the blackboard, but they have come back years later to tell me that they have never had trouble spelling the word after seeing my illustration.

Of course, the following list of entries is not exhaustive, but it shows you how to conjure up mental pictures or letter patterns to aid you in spelling. In addition to this list, you should start your own collection of words you have trouble spelling. As you add words to your list, underline the most troublesome letters in the word. Then think up a picture or look for a pattern to help you visualize the correct spelling in your own mind. Applying this technique consistently, you will eventually become a competent speller.

A

ABANDON is spelled just like the three words **a band on**. Think of *a band on* a desert island whose members have been abandoned.

A **BAND** ON

ABDOMEN has the word **dome** in the middle of it. Picture a man with a dome in his middle.

ABSENCE ends in **-ce**, not **-se**. Remember that students with many absences end up with a grade of *C* (or worse!).

ABUNDANCE ends **-dance**. It is spelled just like the three words *a bun dance*.

ABUNDANCE

A BUN DANCE

ABYSS has a **y** in the middle. Picture the *y* as a deep abyss within the word.

An **ACCIDENT** leaves a **dent** in the end.

ACCOMMODATE begins with **a** and ends with **-date**. In between are three pairs of letters, *c*'s, *m*'s, and *o*'s. Think of those *c*'s, *m*'s, and *o*'s as couples out on a date—all three in pairs.

A^{CC}O_{MM}ODATE

ADDRESS has two **d**'s. The address is what you **add** to the letter before you mail it.

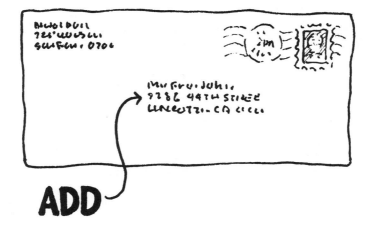

ADVERTISE ends in -**se**, not -*ze.* Remember that the purpose of advertising is to **se**ll, not to "**ze**ll."

ADVICE / ADVISE. *Advice* is a noun, *advise* is a verb. Compare these to **rice** and **rise**. *Rice* is a noun, a thing, while *rise* is a verb, an action. (The same holds true for *device* and *devise.*)

NOUNS	VERBS
R**ICE**	R**ISE**
AD**VICE**	AD**VISE**
DE**VICE**	DE**VISE**

THE CHEF WATCHED THE
RICE RISE

ALIEN begins with **a lie**. Watch out for *a lie* when you first meet an *alie*n.

ALTAR (a ceremonial table) ends -**ar**. Think of the *Arch*bishop who might stand before it.

ALTER (to change) ends -**er**. Think of the word *erase.* To al**ter** something, you **er**ase the original.

AL**TAR**	AL**TER**
ARCHBISHOP	**ER**ASE

AMATEUR begins with the words **a mate**. Think of an amateur golfer who learns the game by practicing with his or her spouse, or mate.

An **AMBULANCE** has **Lance** hanging off the back!

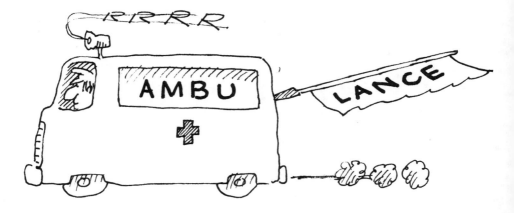

ANGEL ends -**el**. An ang*el* lives at a high *el*evation.

ANGLE, the bend formed by the meeting of two lines, ends in -**le**. Think of a *le*g, which bends at the knee to form an an-g*le*.

ANOINT is spelled with one **n** after the **a**. To *anoint* someone is to pour *an oint*ment over his or her head.

AN**OINT** (MENT)

A Matter of Some **Ant**ics

Some of the most commonly misspelled words are those that sound as if they end with *-ent* but that actually end with **-ant**: *pregnant, fragrant, vagrant,* and *defendant.* When you run across such a word, try to imagine ants being or doing what the word describes.

VAGR**ANT**   REPENT**ANT**

FRAGR**ANT**   RELUCT**ANT**

TRU**ANT**   RADI**ANT**

OBSERV**ANT** SERGE**ANT**   PREGN**ANT**

DEFEND**ANT**   INF**ANT**

DEFEND**ANT**

Don't forget the first **c** in **ARCTIC**. The **arc**tic is the area north of the polar *arc.*

ARDUOUS has a **duo** in the middle. Think of some ar*duo*us task, such as mountain climbing, that is best undertaken by no less than two.

ARGUMENT drops the *e* in *argue* before adding *-ment*. Remember that argument has **gum** in the middle.

AR GUM ENT

ARTILLERY. One finds **tiller**, like a *tiller* of the soil, in the middle of ar*tillery*.

ASCENT with a **c** is the act of *c*limbing.

ASSENT with an **ss** is to *s*ay *s*o, to agree to or affirm.

```
             B        A S S E N T
         M            A O
       I              Y
     L
 A S C E N T
```

ASCERTAIN is spelled like the two words **as certain.** To *ascertain* something is to be *as certain* as possible about it.

ATTENDANCE ends -**DANCE.** Remember that most students like to *attend a dance.*

attend

atten**dance**

dance

ATTEN**DANCE**

AUGER with an **-er** is a bor*er*, a tool for boring holes.

AUGUR with an **-ur** is one who tries to read the future, like a guru. An *augur* shows up in the middle of an in*augur*ation, because everyone hopes that new leadership *augurs* well for the future.

B

BADMINTON. In this game, a **bad** shot is one that goes **into** the net.

BALANCE ends -**ance**, not -*ence*. Think of a knight using his *lance* to keep his ba*lance*.

BA**LANCE**

BALLOON has two l's to go with its two **o**'s. Think of the *o*'s as balloons, each with its own string.

BALL   N

A **BARGAIN** is something that ends in a **gain** for the buyer.

BARRAGE is spelled just like the two words **bar** and **rage**.

A **BATTALION** goes into **batt**le. And battalion has two *t*'s and one *l* just like ba*ttl*e.

A **BEACH** with **ea** is by the *sea*.

A **BEECH** with **ee** is a tr*ee*.

BEECH	BEACH
TREE	SEA

A **BEGGAR** tries to **gar**ner loose change from passersby.

BEG**GAR**

GARNER

BELEAGUER contains the word **league**. When you are be-*league*red, it feels as if you have the whole *league* against you.

BE**LEAGUE**R

Be careful about your **BELIEFS** as well as those people you **BELIEVE** in. Both *believe* and *belief* have a **lie** in the middle!

A **BERG** is another name for an ice**berg**, a mountain of ice. Think of Ev*er*est.

A **BURG** is a city or town. Think of **ur**ban.

B**ER**G	B**UR**G
EV**ER**EST	**UR**BAN

BURG ON BERG

BESEECH has three **e**'s. It is an old word meaning "to seek help or favor."

BES**EE**CH

S**EE**K

BLEAK ends *-eak*, not *-eek*. Notice that *bleak* has a **leak** in the end. Things are indeed b*leak* when there is a *leak* in the end.

BOUNDARY contains an **ar**. A *boundary* contains the *area* enclosed.

BOUND**AR**Y

AREA

BOUNDARY

BREACH with an **ea** refers to a break. Breach of promise means breaking one's promise.

BREECH with an **ee** refers to the back end or something to cover the back end, such as knee breeches.

BREADTH ends **-dth**, just like the other dimension—wi*dth*.

BREA**DTH**

WI**DTH**

BRIDAL with a **-dal** refers to a bride standing at the *al*tar to be married.

BRIDLE with a **-dle** is for riding a horse, as is a sad*dle*.

BRIDAL	**BRI**DLE**
ALTAR	SAD**DLE**

BRIDAL's BRIDLE

BUDGET ends -**get**. Sometimes you have to bud*get* your funds to *get* what you really want.

BULLETIN is spelled just like the two words **bullet in**. You will certainly hear a news *bulletin* if someone fires a *bullet in* the vicinity of the White House.

BULLETIN

BULWARK. A *bulwark* is a big **bulk** with **war** in the middle of it.

BURGLAR ends **-lar**, not *-ler*. A burg*lar* is one who commits *lar*-ceny, or theft.

BURG**LAR**

LARCENY

Many burglars are armed

BUSINESS, with an **i**, is for making *i*ncome.

BUSYNESS with a **y** is just being bus*y*.

BUS **I** NESS   BUS**Y**
N   BUS**Y**NESS
C
O
M
E

BUTTE has two **t**'s.

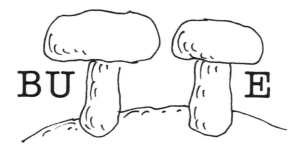

C

CABARET. Picture, if you will, a **cat** that is **bare** in the middle.

BARE

CA∧T

CAFETERIA begins **cafe**-; just like *café*.

A **CALENDAR** ends -**dar**. Remember that a calen*dar* is for marking *days* and *dates*.

DAYS

CALEN**DAR**

DATES

CALORIE ends **-ie** as in d*ie*t. Beginning a low-calor*ie* d*ie*t means eating fewer calor*ie*s.

CALOR**IE**

DIET

CALOR**IE**
D**IE**T

CAPITOL ends **-ol** when referring to that building called the statehouse. All other uses are spelled capit*al*. Think of the *o* as the dome in the capit*ol* building.

CAPSIZE is spelled like the two words **cap** and **size**.

CARESS has one **r** and two **s**'s. Ca*r*e*ss* begins with *care*.

CASUALTIES is spelled like the two words **casual** and **ties**.

CATEGORY is in a category all by itself because it begins cate-, not cata-. Think of the word having a big **ego** in the middle because it is not like *catacomb, cataclysm,* and *catatonic*.

CEMETERY. Strangely enough, *cemetery* has a **meter** in the middle of it.

CE**METER**Y

CHASTISE ends -**se**, not -ze. Remember that *chasti**se*** is another word for **s**cold.

CHASTI**S**E
　　　　　C
　　　　　O
　　　　　L
　　　　　D

CHOOSE is present tense, when you select now.

CHOSE is past tense, when you have already selected.

A **CHORD** is a combination of notes played in harmony. Remember the *h* that begins *h*armony.

A **CORD,** with four letters, is a rope, another word with four letters.

CHORD	CORD
A	ROPE
R	
M	
O	
N	
Y	

To **CITE** something with a **c** is to *c*all it to mind.

To **SIGHT** something refers to seeing it with one's eye**sight**.

A **SITE** is where something **sit**s, where it is *sit*uated on the terrain.

CLIMATIC conditions, from the word clim**ate**, depend on where you are **at** on the globe.

CLIMACTIC moments are turning points, like the key **act** in a drama where the plot reaches its climax.

COLLAR ends **-ar**, not *-er*. In police jargon, a coll*ar* is an *ar*rest.

COLL**AR**

ARREST

COMPARISON has **Paris** in the middle. Is there any com*paris*on to the beauty of *Paris*?

COM**PARIS**ON

COMPETITION. The second vowel is an **e** as in comp**e**te. Visualize your **pet** turtle in the middle of com*pet*ition—the annual turtle race.

COMPLIMENT / COMPLEMENT. A compliment is a flattering remark. Think, "*I* like being in the middle of a compl*i*ment." A compl**e**ment completes something (His tie complements his shirt.), and like *complete,* it is spelled with two *e*'s.

COMPL**I**MENT **COMPLE**MENT

COMPLETE

L
I
K
E

I
T

CONQUEROR ends -**or**, not -*er*. Conquerors may feel they must conquer *or* be conquered.

CONQUER**OR**

CONQUER **OR** BE CONQUERED

CONSCIENCE. Science comes from the Latin word *scientia,* which means "having knowledge." The word con*science* has *science* in it, which makes sense because con*science* is "the knowledge within."

CONSPIRACY ends -*acy*. It is spelled like two words, **cons** and **piracy**. Think of some *cons* (convicts) engaged in a *conspiracy* to commit *piracy*.

CONTEMPORARY has **tempo** in it. To be con*tempo*rary is to be in the swing of things, to be in touch with the *tempo* of the times.

CON**TEMPO**RARY

CONTROVERSY. Poor old **Rover** is always at the center of con-*trover*sy.

CONVENIENT. On a see-saw, it is most con**veni**ent when the weight is equal on each side. Picture *convenient* with those -*en*'s on each side of the *i*.

conv **EN**   **EN** t

I

CONVERTIBLE ends **-ible**, not *-able*. Think to yourself "**I** wish **I** were sitting in a convertible."

CORRESPONDENCE ends **-ence**. When you have finished writing your correspond*e*nce, you put it in an *e*nvelope.

COWARD, like *backward*, ends with **-ward**. Co*wards* are those who run back*wards* when the battle begins.

CRATER ends **-ter**, not *-tor*. A cra*ter* is a bowl-shaped depression in the *ter*rain.

CRA**TER** in the **TER**RAIN

CRITICISM ends *-cism*. Sometimes criticism arises because the **critic is m**ad at someone.

CRITIC IS MAD
CRITIC IS M

CROCODILE is spelled with an *o* in the middle. Picture a crocodile with a **cod** inside of it.

CRO**COD**ILE

CUPBOARD. Don't be misled by its pronunciation. A *cupboard* is simply a **board**, or cabinet, where **cup**s are stored.

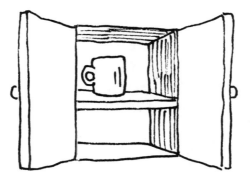

A **CURRANT** is a sweet, raisin-like fruit that might attract **ants**. Curr*ent* is the spelling of *every* other use.

CURR**ANT**   CURR**ENT**
       N   V
       T   E
       S   R
                   Y
                   T
                   H
                   I
                   N
                   G
                   E
                   L
                   S
                   E

CYMBALS are brass discs banged together to make a **c**rashing sound during the **ba**nd concert.

SYMBOLS are **S**ignificant images, or **S**igns, such as one finds in a *book*.

CYM**BAL**   **S**YMBOL
R   **BAND**   I   **BO**OK
A   G
S   N
H

D

DEFENSE is spelled with an **s**, not a *c*. Think of *defense* as keeping things *safe* and *sound*. (Actually, the British spell defense with a *c*, but they can write their own spelling books.)

DEFEN**S**E
    A
    F
    E

DELEGATE begins *dele-*, not *dela-*. The word **leg** appears in the center of de*leg*ate. Picture a convention of long-*leg*ged basketball players.

DEMAGOGUE begins *dema-*, not *demo-*. The word **agog** appears in the middle of dem*agog*ue. Think of a crowd all *agog* at some demagogue's spell-binding oration.

DEPENDENT ends *-dent*, not *-dant*. Children are called depen**dent**s because they put a major *dent* in the family budget.

DESCENDANT ends *-ant*. The opposite of descend**ant** is **an**cestor, both words containing *an*.

ANCESTOR
DESCENDANT

DESCEND**ANT**

> **DISCREET** means "careful, discerning." *Discreet* people, those who are careful, are at ease together, so keep those *e*'s together in *discreet*.
>
> **DISCRETE** means "separate" or "distinct," so let's do what the word says and keep the *e*'s separate in discr**ete**.

DISILLUSIONMENT. *Disillusion* originally meant to lose one's illusions. Remember that there is an **illusion** in the middle of dis*illusion*ment.

DISSECT has two **s**'s, as if the *s* itself were di*ss*ected.

DISTURBANCE ends *-ance*. Notice there is a **turban** in the middle of dis*turban*ce.

DIVIDE begins **di**- not *de*-. Think of a letter *i* that gets di*v*ided by a sharp edged *v*.

DUEL / DUAL. *Duel* with an **e** is a fight between two enemies. *Dual* with an **a** is used for all other references to two of something.

```
DUEL      DUAL
   N         L
   E         L
   M
   I         O
   E         T
   S         H
             E
             R
```

E

ELEGANT. The first vowel, the *e*, is easy, but the other two vowels are often switched around. Remember that *elegant* is another *-ant* word, this time an **ant** with its **leg** in front.

E **LEG ANT**

ELICIT / ILLICIT. To *elicit* is to draw out or **e**voke something; *illicit* is something **i**mproper or **i**llegal.

E L I C I T
V O K E

ILL I C I T
E G A L

EMIGRATE is to exit from a country, to migrate out.

IMMIGRATE is to migrate into a country.

Emigrate has one **m**; *immigrate* has two. Think of the *m*'s as *migrants*. In the U.S. there are at least twice as many people trying to get into the country as there are trying to exit, so the two *m*'s go with the immigrants.

EMPHASIZE ends in **-size**, a good way to empha*size* a point.

ENDORSE begins with an *e*, not an *i*. Remember that you endorse a check by writing your name on the back at one **end**.

ENTERPRISE also begins with an *e*, not an *i*, and ends -*se*, not -*ze*. An **enter**pri**se** often involves *enter*ing into the business of *se*lling.

ENTER INTO **SE**LLING

ENTER PRI **SE**

ENTOURAGE has both an *o* and a *u*. Notice the word **tour** in the middle. A performer's en*tour*age consists of the people who go on *tour* with him or her.

ENVIRONMENT has the word **iron** in it, just as the mineral *iron* exists in our natural env*iron*ment.

EQUATOR ends **-tor**, not *-ter*. Mapmakers call the hot region around the equator the *Torr*id Zone.

EQUA**TOR**

TORRID ZONE

-ERY VS. **-ARY**. One way to tell whether a word ends *-ery* or *-ary* is to ask if the word is related to an occupation, naming a kind of work**er**.

A BAK**ER** bakes bread at a BAK**ERY**.

A BIND**ER** binds books at a BIND**ERY**.

A GROC**ER** sells food at a GROC**ERY**.

A HOSI**ER** sells hose (stockings) called HOSI**ERY**.

EVAPORATION is the process of a liquid turning to **vapor**, so it should come as no surprise that *vapor* is in the middle of e*vapor*ation.

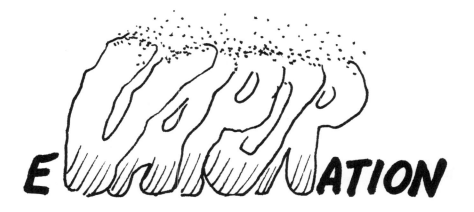

EXALT/EXULT. *Exalt* means elevating someone or something, holding them up for praise or esteem. The **-alt** ending comes from the same root as *alt*itude, or height. *Exult*, which ends **-ult**, means to rejoice in a lively way, as if you've experienced the *ult*imate thrill in life.

EX**ALT**   EX**ULT**

ALTITUDE   **ULT**IMATE THRILL

EXULT

EXCELLENT has two *l*'s followed by an *e*. The name **Ellen** appears in the middle of the word. Notice, however, that *Ellen* is also in the middle of rep*ellen*t! Think, "*Ellen* has invented an exc*ellen*t insect rep*ellen*t."

EXCELLENT REPELLENT

EXERCISE ends -*se*, not -*ce*. Associate the **s** with the *s*weat that often goes with exercise.

EXERCI S E
W
E
A
T

EXPENSE ends *-se*, not *-ce*. Think of the *s* as a dollar sign ($) with which expenses are measured.

EXPEN$E

EXTRAORDINARY. Though the *a* gets lost in pronunciation, *extraordinary* is simply **extra ordinary**, out of the ordinary.

F

FAMILIAR. Don't forget that second *i*. *Familiar* ends with the word **liar**.

FAMI**LIAR**

FARCE has a **c**, not an **s**. A farce is a kind of comedy.

FAR**C**E
O
M
E
D
Y

FEBRUARY is sometimes pronounced without the first *r*, like *Febuary*. Remember to include both *r*'s, so that you can spell **brr** in the month of Fe*bruary*.

FRIEND follows the "*i*- before -*e*" rule, and so ends with -*end*. A good fri**end** will stay with you to the very **end**.

FLUORESCENT does not begin like *flour*. (Would you want to eat bread that glows in the dark?) But it does have **ores** in the middle. Think of rock museums displaying mineral ores that glow in the dark.

FORTY is the age at which some people feel they have lost their youth. So lose the **U**th in *four* to make forty.

FOREWORD / FORWARD. A *foreword* is the preface in a book that comes be**fore** the **words** in the main text. *Forward* ends -**ward** like its opposite, back*ward*.

FORE	**WORD**	FOR**WARD**
BE**FORE** THE OTHER **WORDS**		BACK**WARD**

FORE- WORDS.   We use the word *before* in reference to time (She arrived *before* noon.) and in reference to space (He stood *before* the king.). If you are trying to figure out whether a word begins *for-* or *fore-*, first decide if either meaning of *before* is involved in the definition of the word you are trying to spell. If it is, begin the word with *fore-*.

BEFORE ("prior in time")

FORECAST	**FORE**SEEABLE
FOREFATHER	**FORE**SHADOW
FOREGONE	**FORE**THOUGHT
FORERUNNER	**FORE**WARN

BEFORE ("in front")

FOREARM	**FORE**HEAD
FOREHAND	**FORE**MAN

FOUL/FOWL. *Fowl* with a *w* refers to birds (such as an **owl**). *Foul* with a *u* refers to something **out** of **bou**nds, whether on the playing field or *out*side the b**ou**nds of good taste.

FOWL FOUL

OWL   OUT OF

BOUNDS

F**OWL**

F**OUL**
OUT OF
BOUNDS

FOUNTAIN ends **-ain**. The falling droplets of water from a fountain are almost like r**ain**.

FOUNT**AIN**

R**AIN**

"FUL" WORDS. *Full* is a **full** word all by itself. But when attached, *full* is no longer **full**, since it loses an *l*.

art**ful**	**ful**fill
aw**ful**	**ful**some
beauti**ful**	help**ful**
cup**ful**	right**ful**
dread**ful**	wonder**ful**

G

GARBAGE is spelled with **bag** in it, like when the gar*bage* over-flows the *bag*.

GAR**BAG**E

GAUGE begins *ga-*, not *gu-*. One may find a **ga**uge attached to a **ga**dget, and the spelling of the two starts out the same way.

GAUGE

GADGET

GENEALOGY. Though it's pronounced like all those other studies ending in *-ology,* gene**a**logy has *al* in the middle, not *ol*. Think of researching your family tree, and don't forget to include Uncle **Al**.

GOVERNMENT. The *n* sometimes gets lost in pronunciation. Still, a gover**n**ment has a responsibility to gover*n*.

GOVER**N**MENT

GOVER**N**

GRAMMAR ends **-mar**. Remember that a *ram* bumps *ma* in the middle of g*rammar*.

G **RAM MA** R

GUARD begins **gu-**, not *ga-*. Remember that a *gu*ard sometimes carries a *gu*n, and the two words begin the same way.

GUARD

GUN

H

HAMBURGER is spelled *burg*, not *berg*. Notice the word **urge** in the middle of hamb*urge*r. People often have an *urge* for a hamb*urge*r.

HAMB**URGE**R

HANGAR / HANGER. A hanger for clothes is spelled just the way it sounds. But a hangar for airplanes ends **-gar**. You can remember that by thinking of a han*gar* as a *gar*age for airplanes.

HAN**GAR**

GARAGE for AIRPLANES

HARBOR ends *-bor*, not *-ber*. Remember that a har**bo**r is for **bo**ats.

HAR**BOR**

BOATS

HEIGHT ends with the word **eight**. A person who is *eight* feet tall certainly has h*eight*.

I

IDLE / IDOL. Being id**le**, not engaged in any activity, may be associated with **le**thargy, lack of energy. An id**ol**, an image of a god, is associated with **ol**d deities and **ol**d religions.

ID**LE**   ID**OL**

   LETHARGY   **OL**D RELIGIONS

IMPLY / INFER. When an author or speaker **imp**lies something, a hidden meaning is *imp*lanted. When a reader or listener in**fers** something, he or she *fer*rets out the meaning of what someone else has said.

IMPLY

IMPLANTED BY THE AUTHOR

IN**FER**

   FERRETED OUT BY THE READER

IMPRUDENT ends *-ent*, not *-ant*. Notice the word **rude** in im-p*rude*nt. Being *rude* is usually imp*rude*nt.

INCENSE ends *-se*, not *-ce*. Incense is fragrant **s**moke.

INCEN**SE**

INCUMBENT ends with the word **bent**. Think of politicians who have been in office so long that they are decrepit and *bent* over.

INCUM**BENT**

INCUM **BENT**

INDEBTED contains an unsounded *b*. One usually becomes indebted by **b**orrowing something.

<pre>
INDE**B**TED
      O
      R
      R
      O
      W
      I
      N
      G
</pre>

INDISPENSABLE ends with -**sable**. Picture a wealthy couple who simply couldn't live without their *sable* furs.

INDULGENT ends -**gent**. Picture an aristocratic *gent* who is very indul*gent*.

INDUL**GENT**

INNOVATION is spelled just like the two words **inn** and **ovation**. Think of a fine hotel or *inn*, with all the latest innovations, which earns an *ovation* from its guests.

INTERRUPT has two *r*'s. Notice the word **err** in the middle. If you int*err*upt someone, you *err* in etiquette.

INTERVENE ends **-ene**. An *n* interv*ene*s between the last two *e*'s.

INTIMATE ends *-mate*. A person you are inti**mate** with is your **mate**.

INTI **MATE**

-IS / -ES ENDINGS.   We all know that **this** refers to something singular and **these** to something plural. In other words as well, *-is* endings are singular and *-es* endings are plural.

TH**IS**	TH**ES**E
THES**IS**	THES**ES**
ANALYS**IS**	ANALYS**ES**
HYPOTHES**IS**	HYPOTHES**ES**
NEUROS**IS**	NEUROS**ES**

ITS / IT'S. The confusion between these two words produces a common misspelling.

It's is the contraction of **it is**. The apostrophe stands for a missing letter, just as it does in *don't, shouldn't,* or *you're*.

Its is the possessive form of **it**. Just as *his* and *hers* do not have apostrophes, neither should *its*.

K

KNOWLEDGE is spelled like the two words **know** and **ledge**. *Knowledgeable* is spelled like the three words **know**, **ledge**, and **able**.

KNOWLEDGEABLE = **KNOW** THE **LEDGE**
IS AVOID**ABLE**

L

LABEL ends -*el*. Think of a la*bel* with **abe** in the middle.

LABOR ends in **-or**. Lab*or* is another word for w*or*k.

LAB**OR**

W**OR**K

LABORATORY has four vowels. Think of a **lab orator**, speaking to his fellow scientists. (And if you can't remember how to spell o*rat*ory, look for the *rat* inside.)

LAB**ORATOR**Y

LESSEN / LESSON. To make something less is to **lessen** it— *less* + *-en*. A **lesson** is something you might teach your **son**.

LETTUCE ends **-uce**. Lett*uce* is one kind of prod*uce*.

LETT**UCE**

PROD**UCE**

LIBRARY has two *r*'s. Think of a library with a **ra** in the middle.

LICENSE ends *-se*, not *-ce*. In most states, **s**ixteen is the age one can acquire a driver's license.

LICEN**SE**

I

X

T

E

E

N

LIEUTENANT. This word can be creatively misspelled in any number of ways. Visualize an ant lieutenant ordering ten young recruits to hit the dirt. He is barking to ten dazed ant privates, **"Lie, u ten ants!"**

LITERATURE. The preferred pronunciation of this word includes all four syllables: lit-er-a-ture. Note the **era** in the middle. Many classic works of lit*era*ture take us to another *era*.

$$\text{LIT}^{\textbf{ERA}}\text{TURE}$$

LONELINESS. Don't forget that first *e*. *Loneliness* begins with the word **lone**. A *lone* survivor might well experience *lone*liness.

LONELINESS

LONE SURVIVOR

LOOSE with two *o*'s is the opposite of *tight* or *bound*. *Lose* with one *o* is the opposite of *find* or *win*. **Loose** rhymes with m**oose** and ends with the same letters. Just remember, "The m*oose* is l*oose*!"

M

MANAGER is spelled like **man** and **ager**. Being a manager can be a job that makes one old before his time—that is, a real *man ager*.

MAN**AGER**

MANTEL / MANTLE. A *mantel*, ending **-el**, is a she*l*f over a fireplace. The *mantle* you wear ends with **e**, like the cape that it is.

```
MANTEL              C
        SHELF       A
                    P
              MANTLE
```

MANUAL / MANUEL. *Manual*, ending **-al**, refers to the hand, either hand labor or a handbook. *Manuel*, ending **-el**, is the hispanic name, **e***l nombre hispanico*.

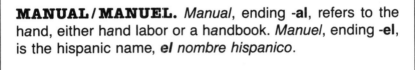

```
           H
  MANUAL       MANUEL
           N         El nombre
           D
```

MARRIAGE. Don't forget the **i**. The *y* in *marry* turns to *i* in *marriage*. Remember, mar**ri**age should never end in *rage*!

MATERIAL / MATERIEL. *Materiel*, ending **-el**, refers to the equipment of an organization. It is most often used in reference to military weapons and supplies. *Material*, the more general word, is used for **all** other meanings.

```
MATERIEL        MATERIAL
        Q           ALL OTHER USES
        U
        I
        P
        M
        E
        N
        T
```

MAXIMUM　　**MINIMUM**

MEAGER includes **eager**. Think of store clerks whose m*eager* salaries make them *eager* for a raise.

MEDAL / METAL / MEDDLE. A *medal* with a **d** is a *d*isk to *d*ecorate *d*oers of *d*istinguished *d*eeds. *Metals* are mineral elements such as *t*in, copper, gold, and the like. *Meddle* is a verb—to intrude into the mi*dd*le of someone else's business.

ME**D**AL	ME**T**AL	ME**DD**LE = get into the
E	I	MI**DD**LE
C	N	
O		
R	E	
A	T	
T	C	
I		
V		
E		
D		
I		
S		
K		

MEDALLION has one *d* and two *l*'s, like the two words **medal** and **lion**.

MEDIEVAL contains the word **die** in the middle. The plague and the crusades caused many people to *die* in the middle of the me*die*val era.

ME**DIE**VAL

DIE

MEMENTO begins **mem**-, not *mom*-. A *mem*ento helps you re-*mem*ber an important occasion.

MEMENTO

RE**MEM**BER

MENACE is spelled like the two words **men** and **ace**. Think of the *menace* that would occur if all the *men* playing poker have *aces*.

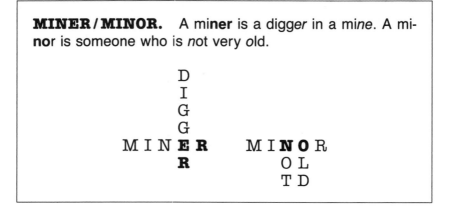

MINER/MINOR. A miner is a digger in a mine. A minor is someone who is not very old.

```
        D
        I
        G
        G
M I N   E R        M I N O R
        R                O L
                         T D
```

MINOR **MINER**

MISSPELL has two s's. Don't miss that second s in misspell.

MOSQUITOES. The preferred spelling ends -*es*. Mosqui**toes** keep you on your *toes*.

MOSQUI**TOES**

MOTOR ends **-or**. A mo*tor* produces *tor*que.

MO**TOR**
TORQUE

MOUNTAIN ends **-ain** just like its opposite, the pl*ain*.

MOUNT**AIN**

PL**AIN**

MUSCLE. You can remember the spelling of this word if you've ever seen a T-shirt worn by athletes at the **U**niversity of **S**outhern **C**alifornia (USC).

N

NAVAL / NAVEL. Nava*l*, ending **-al**, refers to ships and sailors, like nautica*l*. Nave*l* ending **-el**, refers to the be*l*ly button.

NAV**AL**	NAV**EL**
NAUTIC**AL**	B**EL**LY BUTTON

NAVAL's NAVEL

NORMAL ends *-al*. It's spelled like the names **Norm** and **Al**.

NUCLEAR. Despite its common mispronunciation (NUKE-u-ler), *nuclear* is pronounced *NU-klee-er* and spelled like un**clear** with the first two letters reversed.

It is UN**CLEAR** to many whether or not

NU**CLEAR** power is the energy of the future.

O

OBSCENE. Someone who is ob**scene** may end up creating quite a *scene*.

OB**SCENE**

OFFENSE, like defense, ends *-se,* not *-ce.* In sports, the offense usually tries to **s**core point**s**.

```
OFFENSE   P
      C   O
      O   I
      R   N
     ET   S
```

OPPRESSION.   Unlike *depress* and *repress*, *oppress* has two
p's, not one. Think of o**pp**ression as *p*ersistent *p*ersecution.

```
O P P R E S S I O N
  E E
  R R
  S S
  I E
  S C
  T U
  E T
  N I
  T O
    N
```

An **ORNAMENT** has a **name** inside.

P

A **PAGODA** has **a god** in the middle.

PARISH / PERISH.   A **par**ish is a church community served by a *par*son or priest. To **per**ish, or be "wiped out," is to be *er*adicated.

PARISH	**PER**ISH
PARSON	**ER**ADICATED

PASSED / PAST. Passed is any action of passing which has already occurred. Pa*st* is a reference to *tense* or to *times* gone by. "In the pa*st* week Congress pa*ss*ed three bills."

PASSED =

ACT OF **PASS**ING WHICH ALREADY OCCURRED

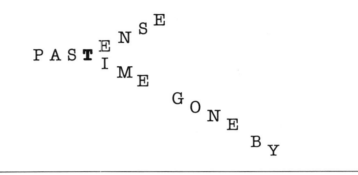

IN THE **PAST** HE
PASSED THE BALL

PATIENCE / PATIENTS. Patience is the trait of calm endurance. Patients are the clients of a doctor or dentist. Patients at a clinic must often have patience.

```
P A T I E N  C  E        PATIENT
             A  N        CLIENT
             L  D
             M  U
                R
                A
                N
                C
                E
```

PENALTY. Imagine a player named **Al** in the middle of the penalty box.

PERMANENT has an *a* in the middle and an *e* in the last syllable. Notice the **mane** in the middle of a per*mane*nt.

> **PERSONAL / PERSONNEL.** *Personnel* refers to the peo-
> ple working for a particular company, or to their names on a
> list. *Personal* refers to *all* other uses relating to a person.
>
> ```
> P E R S O N N E L  PERSONAL
>           A M I              ALL OTHER USES
>           M P S
>           E L T
>           S O
>             Y
>           O E
>           N E
> ```

PHENOMENON ends with the three words **no men on**. A baseball pitcher is considered a phenomenon if there are *no men on* base during an entire game.

PHONY has no *e*. It is spelled like **pony** with an added **h**. Think of a p*h*ony pony.

PIGEON is spelled like the words **pig** and **eon**. Visualize, if you must, a *pig* who after an *eon* evolves into a *pigeon*.

PILGRIM ends -*im*. Imagine a pil**grim** enduring a *grim* winter in a new land.

GRIM
PIL**GRIM**

PILLAR ends -**ar**. A pill*ar* is a component of *ar*chitecture.

PILL**AR**
ARCHITECTURE

PLAYWRIGHTS may *write* and their dramas may be all *right*. But they are named **wrights** because they shape and fashion their works as do wheel*wrights* and cart*wrights*. The same verb—*wright*—gives us *wrought*, something fashioned with effort into a particular shape.

WHEEL**WRIGHT**   PLAY**WRIGHT**

POLAR ends -*ar*. Pol*ar* bears and other pol*ar* things are associated with the *ar*ctic.

POL**AR**
ARCTIC

POPULAR ends *-lar*, not *-ler*. To be popu*lar* means you have a *lar*ge fan club.

POPU**LAR**

LARGE FAN CLUB

POTATOES and **TOMATOES** both have **toes**!

POTA**TOES**   TOMA**TOES**

PRAY / PREY.   To pray involves asking God for something. Prey involves hunting and killing something to eat.

PR**A**Y   PR**E**Y
S   A
K   T
I   I
N   N
G   G

PRECEDENT derives from precede, that which comes earlier.

PRESIDENT, the one who steers an institution, derives from preside.

```
P R E C E D E N T          P R E S I D E N T
    A A                        T N
    M R                        E S
    E L                        E T
      I                        R I
      E                        S T
      R                          U
                                 T
                                 I
                                 O
                                 N
```

PREPARATION is the act of *preparing*. It retains the middle **a** in prepare.

```
PREPARATION
PREPARE
```

PRETENSE ends -*se*, not -*ce*. A pretense is basically a *sham*.

```
PRETENSE
      H
      A
      M
```

> **PRINCIPAL / PRINCIPLE.** *Princip*le is a noun referring to some fundamental ru*le*, law, or standard of conduct such as moral princip*le*s. **All** other uses, whether nouns or adjectives, are spelled *princip*al, referring to someone or something of first importance: a school princip*al*; princip*al* parts; princip*al*s in a business deal; the princip*al* on a loan.
>
> PRINCIP**LE**   PRINCIP**AL**
>
>   RU**LE**   **AL**L OTHER USES

PRINCIPAL's PRINCIPLE

PROFESSOR has one **f** and two **s**'s. A professor should pro*fess* to know his or her field.

PURSUE is spelled like **purse** with an extra **u** added. *"U"* might *pursue* a *purse*-snatcher.

R

RASPBERRY is spelled as if each berry were a **rasp**.

RASPBERRY

RECOMMEND is simply *re-* + *commend*. If you have commended someone's work, you can *re*commend him or her to other employers.

REHEARSAL has *hear* in the middle. A conductor re**hear**ses a symphony orchestra so that he or she can **hear** how it sounds.

REINDEER is just the two words **rein** and *deer*. Santa puts *reins* on this kind of deer to have them pull his sl*ei*gh.

R**EI**NDEER

SL**EI**GH

REMINISCENT could be the title of an unusual memo—**re: mini scent**.

RENOWN may be short-lived in today's world. Famous today, forgotten tomorrow, as the word *renown* reminds us with *now* in the middle.

RE**NOW**N

REPETITION does what it says. First there is a repetition of **e**'s, then a repetition of **i**'s.

R**EPE**T**IT**ION

Your **RESIDENCE** is where you **reside**.

RESIDENCE

RESIDE

RESTAURANT has the word **aura** in the middle. A popular res-
t*aura*nt usually has a special atmosphere or *aura* about it.

The **REVEREND** is one whom the people of the church **revere**.
But if the sermon goes on too long, the congregation may remember that *reverend* also rhymes with *never end*.

REVERE

REVEREND

NEVER END

RIDICULOUS begins *ri-*, not *re-*. **Rid**iculous notions are ones you want to get *rid* of.

RODENT ends -**dent**. A ro*dent* can put a *dent* in the cheese.

ROTOR, like motor, ends -**tor**, not *-ter*. The ro*tor* in a mo*tor* produces *tor*que.

RO**TOR**

TORQUE

MO**TOR**

S

A **SACRILEGIOUS** person is "not religious," and *sacrilegious* is not spelled like *religious* either, because the *e* and *i* are reversed. Notice the word **rile** in the middle. A sac*rile*gious remark will *rile* the devout.

SAC**RILE**GIOUS

SANDAL ends -*al*. After wearing sand*al*s, you may find sand **all** over your feet.

SAND**AL**

SAND **AL**L OVER YOUR FEET

SATELLITE has one *t* and two *l*'s. *Satellite* has the word **tell** in the middle. From its orbit high in space, a sa*tell*ite can *tell* us much more about the world.

SCARED / SCARRED. *Scared* (afraid) has one *r*. *Scarred* has two. After you've been scared once, you may be scarred for life.

SECRETARY begins with the word **secret**. A good secretary is discreet with confidential information and knows how to keep a *secret*.

Both **SEGREGATION** and **CONGREGATION** have a fellow named **Greg** in the middle.

SE**GREG**ATION   CON**GREG**ATION

In **SEPARATE,** the two *a*'s se*parate* the two **e**'s. Remember, there's **a rat** in sep*arate*.

SHEPHERD ends **-herd**, which makes sense because a shep-*herd* looks after a *herd* of sheep.

SLAUGHTER. As strange as it is, *slaughter* is actually **laughter** with an **s** at the beginning.

SOLAR ends **-ar**. For no good reason, many adjectives referring to heavenly bodies end *-ar* (like st*ar*).

ST**AR**
SOL**AR**
LUN**AR**
STELL**AR**
PLANET**AR**Y

SOLDER. Don't forget the **I**, even though this word is pro-nounced *sodder*. Remember, *solder* is used to make a joint or connection *solider*.

SO**L** DER

SO**LI**DER

SOLDIER ends *-ier*. Notice the word **die** in the middle. A sold*ier* risks having to *die* in battle.

SOVEREIGN ends **-reign**. A sover*eign* is one who *reigns*.

SOVE**REIGN**

STAKE / STEAK.   A st**ea**k is to *eat*, while a st**a**ke is a stick to *stabilize* a tent or to *stab* a vampire.

ST**EA**K	ST**A**KE
EAT	**STA**BILIZE
	STAB

STALACTITE / STALAGMITE. These cave formations which look like petrified icicles may not come up in conversation everyday, but do you remember which is which? Every self-respecting person should know that *stala**ct**ites*, spelled with *ct*, hang from the *c*eiling, or *t*op, while *stala**gm**ites*, with *gm*, rise up from the *g*round in cone-like *m*ounds.

```
S T A L A C T I T E S   S T A L A G M I T E S
          E O                     R O
          I P                     O U
          L                       U N
          I                       N D
          N                       D S
          G
```

STALACTITES

STALAGMITES

STATIONARY / STATIONERY. *Stationary* means "anchored," moving **nary** an inch. *Stationery* is pap**er** purchased from a statio**n**er, a supplier of pap**er** and office supplies.

STATIO**NARY**   STATION**ER**Y

            NARY AN INCH   PAP**ER**

THE **STATIONERY**
WASN'T **STATIONARY**

SURGEON ends with the two words **urge** and **on**. Think of a weary surgeon who must *urge on* his or her medical team after performing surgery all through the night.

SUSPENSE ends *-se*, not *-ce*. When you think of suspen*se*, think of a movie or book with a *scary ending*.

```
S U S P E N S E
          C N
          A D
          R I
          Y N
            G
```

T

TEMPERAMENT. Don't forget the *a*. Note the word **ram** in the middle. Someone with a fiery temperament might actually *ram* those who get in the way.

TEMPE**RAM**ENT

THE SUMMER OF OUR DISCON**TENT.** You can remember the endings of some words by thinking of them happening to or near a **tent**.

INCOMPE**TENT** INADVER**TENT**

PENI**TENT** CO-EXIS**TENT**

DISC ON TENT

THERE / THEIR / THEY'RE.   All three begin **the**-, so everyone should get the first three letters right. It's the endings that are commonly confused.

—*The*re ends just like he*re*, another pronoun of location.

—*The*ir ends with an *r* just like other possessives, you*r*, he*r*, and ou*r*.

—*The*y**'re** ends just like other contractions: yo*u're* = you are; we*'re* = we are.

THERE

THEIR

THEY'RE

THERE	THEIR	THEY'**RE** (they are)
HERE	YOU**R**	YOU'**RE** (you are)
	HE**R**	WE'**RE** (we are)

TOURNAMENT begins with the words **tour** and **name**. Sponsors of a major tennis or golf *tournam*ent hope to attract every big *name* on the *tour*.

TOUR**NAME**NT

TRAGEDY.   In the middle of every **trage**dy, whether theatrical or real-life, there is always some *rage*.

TRAGEDY

U

UPHOLSTERY has a **holster** in the middle. Think of cowboy's chair decorated with guns and holsters.

UP**HOLSTER**Y

V

VICE / VISE.   Vice with a *c* stands for two very different (we hope) concepts. One is for **vic**arious (in place of) representatives (*vice* president, *vice*roy). The other is for **c**orrupt practices.

Vise with an **s** describes a device for *squeezing* or holding something so it won't move.

VILLAIN ends *-ain*. A stereotypical vill**ain** loves to cause p**ain**.

VILL**AIN**

P**AIN**

W

WAGON is spelled like the two words **wag** and **on**. Think of a little girl in her wagon commanding her dog to "*wag on!*"

WAGON

WAILS / WALES / WHALES.   All three sound alike and all start with a **w**. Drop the *w* and you can remember which is which.

- A child **wails** when he or she *ails*.

- In **Wales** one can drink traditional British *ales*.

- **Whales** are an endangered species; we have to work to keep them *hale* and hearty.

WAILS	WALES	WHALES
AILS	ALES	HALE & HEARTY

WARE / WEAR / WHERE.   Here are three more words that sound alike and begin with **w**. Again, drop the *w* and find your clues.

- **Ware**s are *ar*ticles for sale.

- **Wear** goes with t*ear* in the phrase *wear and tear*, and both end *-ear*.

- The question "**where**?" can be answered "*here*."

WARES	WEAR &	WHERE
ARTICLES	TEAR	HERE

WELFARE has only one *l*. Note that **elf** in the middle and think of a little fellow who has hit upon hard times.

Appendix: Patterns of Spelling in American English

It is difficult to learn spelling by the "rules," because there are so many rules and so many exceptions. What is offered here is an overview of the more reliable rules, some of the more predictable spelling regularities of American English.

1. *I* before *E*...

The great and famous spelling rule is

i before *e*
except after *c*
or when sounded like *ay*
as in *neighbor* and *weigh*

This one works for many common words like field, niece, receive, and ceiling. The rule even works for some more unusual words like sleigh and chow mein. But there are a number of qualifications and exceptions.

    a. The rule applies only when the *c* is sounded like *see*. When the *c* is sounded as *sh*, the letters that follow are *ie*, not *ei*. Note, for example, efficient, proficient, and ancient. Science is also spelled *ie*, because again the *c* is not sounded *see*.

    b. The "*i* before *e*..." rule applies after a *see* sound, even when the letter *c* is not actually present: seize, seizure.

c. These words are spelled *ei* even though they do not come after a *see* sound and are not sounded *ay*.

caff*ei*ne	h*ei*ght
cod*ei*ne	l*ei*sure
counterf*ei*t	n*ei*ther
*ei*ther	prot*ei*n
forf*ei*t	sover*ei*gn
h*ei*fer	w*ei*rd

d. These words follow a *see*-sound, yet are spelled *ie*.

fan*ci*er   finan*ci*er   s*ie*ge

2. -CEDE/-CEED/-SEDE

There are scores of verbs that end with the sound *seed*. All of these are spelled -*cede* except for these four:

Three -*seed* verbs end -*ceed*.

suc*ceed*   ex*ceed*   pro*ceed*

Only one -*seed* verb ends -*sede*.

super*sede*.

3. -IFY/-EFY

There are likewise a great number of verbs ending -*ify*. Only four end -*efy*.

lique*fy*	rare*fy*
putre*fy*	stupe*fy*

4. -ND becomes -NSE

When a verb ends -*nd*, some of the words derived from it will substitute *s* for *d*:

def*end*	→	defe*nse*
exp*and*	→	expa*ns*ive
off*end*	→	offe*nse*
pret*end*	→	prete*nse*
susp*end*	→	suspe*ns*eful

5. -DGE ENDINGS

Words ending *-dge* drop the *e* before adding *-ment*.

abri*dge* → abri*dg*ment
acknowle*dge* → acknowle*dg*ment
ju*dge* → ju*dg*ment

6. -ABLE/-IBLE

There are more words ending *-able* than *-ible*, so if it comes to a coin toss, choose *-able*. Generally, *-able* is added to words that could stand alone without a suffix.

agree → agree*able*
break → break*able*
depend → depend*able*
predict → predict*able*

-able also follows word stems ending *i*: appreci*-able*, reli*-able*, soci*-able*.

The ending *-ible* is usually added to word parts that could not stand alone without the suffix.

aud + ible = aud*ible*
cred + ible = cred*ible*
feas + ible = feas*ible*
vis + ible = vis*ible*

Normally, when adding *-able* to a word ending in *-e*, one drops the *e*:

desir*e* + *able* = desir*able*
pleasur*e* + *able* = pleasur*able*
us*e* + *able* = us*able*

7. HARD *C*/SOFT *C*

The letter *c* can be sounded like a *k* (*cash*) or like an *s* (*city*). These are called "hard *c*" and "soft *c*," respectively.

However, if a word ends "soft c + e," retain the e before -able (to retain the "soft c" sound).

notice	noticeable
peace	peaceable
service	serviceable

Word stems ending with a "hard c" sound take the -able suffix.

applicable
despicable
implacable

8. HARD G/SOFT G

Like the letter c, g can be sounded as a "hard g" (gate) or "soft g" (gentleman). The spelling rules regarding hard g/soft g are similar to those concerning hard c/soft c.

Words ending "soft g + e" retain the e before adding -able or -ous (to retain the "soft g" sound).

change	→ changeable	advantage	→ advantageous
knowledge	→ knowledgeable	courage	→ courageous
manage	→ manageable	outrage	→ outrageous

Word stems ending "hard g" add -able:

indefatigable   navigable

Soft g may also be followed by -ible endings:

eligible	negligible
intelligible	tangible

9. *C ENDINGS*

Words ending in c add a k (to retain the "hard c" sound) before adding a suffix.

bivouac	→ bivouacked
frolic	→ frolicking
panic	→ panicking
shellac	→ shellacked

10. Y/EY

In forming plurals, a final *y* preceded by a consonant is usually replaced by *ie* before adding *s*.

baby   → bab*ies*

caddy → cadd*ies*

poppy → popp*ies*

But if the word ends *-ey*, simply add *s*.

alley   → alle*ys*

attorney → attorne*ys*

chimney → chimne*ys*

valley   → valle*ys*

(One exception here is mon*ey* → mon*ies*.)

11. PRIZE/-PRISE

Prize ends *-ze*. But when part of another word, the ending is spelled *-prise*.

com*prise*   enter*prise*   sur*prise*

12. N+NESS

When adding *-ness* to a word already ending with an *n*, retain both *n*'s.

drunke*nn*ess   gree*nn*ess

eve*nn*ess   thi*nn*ess

NTC LANGUAGE ARTS BOOKS

Business Communication
Business Communication Today! *Thomas & Fryar*
Handbook for Business Writing, *Baugh, Fryar, & Thomas*
Meetings: Rules & Procedures, *Pohl*

Dictionaries
British/American Language Dictionary, *Moss*
NTC's Classical Dictionary, *Room*
NTC's Dictionary of Changes in Meaning, *Room*
NTC's Dictionary of Debate, *Hanson*
NTC's Dictionary of Literary Terms, *Morner & Rausch*
NTC's Dictionary of Theatre and Drama Terms, *Mobley*
NTC's Dictionary of Word Origins, *Room*
NTC's Spell It Right Dictionary, *Downing*
Robin Hyman's Dictionary of Quotations

Essential Skills
Building Real Life English Skills, *Starkey & Penn*
English Survival Series, *Maggs*
Essential Life Skills, *Starkey & Penn*
Essentials of English Grammar, *Baugh*
Essentials of Reading and Writing English Series
Grammar for Use, *Hall*
Grammar Step-by-Step, *Pratt*
Guide to Better English Spelling, *Furness*
How to be a Rapid Reader, *Redway*
How to Improve Your Study Skills, *Coman & Heavers*
NTC Skill Builders
Reading by Doing, *Simmons & Palmer*
Developing Creative & Critical Thinking, *Boostrom*
303 Dumb Spelling Mistakes, *Downing*
TIME: We the People, *ed. Schinke-Llano*
Vocabulary by Doing, *Beckert*

Genre Literature
The Detective Story, *Schwartz*
The Short Story & You, *Simmons & Stern*
Sports in Literature, *Emra*
You and Science Fiction, *Hollister*

Journalism
Getting Started in Journalism, *Harkrider*
Journalism Today! *Ferguson & Patten*
Publishing the Literary Magazine, *Klaiman*
UPI Stylebook, *United Press International*

Language, Literature, and Composition
An Anthology for Young Writers, *Meredith*
The Art of Composition, *Meredith*
Creative Writing, *Mueller & Reynolds*

Handbook for Practical Letter Writing, *Baugh*
How to Write Term Papers and Reports, *Baugh*
Literature by Doing, *Tchudi & Yesner*
Lively Writing, *Schrank*
Look, Think & Write, *Leavitt & Sohn*
Poetry by Doing, *Osborn*
World Literature, *Rosenberg*
Write to the Point! *Morgan*
The Writer's Handbook, *Karls & Szymanski*
Writing by Doing, *Sohn & Enger*
Writing in Action, *Meredith*

Media Communication
Getting Started in Mass Media, *Beckert*
Photography in Focus, *Jacobs & Kokrda*
Television Production Today! *Kirkham*
Understanding Mass Media, *Schrank*
Understanding the Film, *Bone & Johnson*

Mythology
The Ancient World, *Sawyer & Townsend*
Mythology and You, *Rosenberg & Baker*
Welcome to Ancient Greece, *Millard*
Welcome to Ancient Rome, *Millard*
World Mythology, *Rosenberg*

Speech
Activities for Effective Communication, *LiSacchi*
The Basics of Speech, *Galvin, Cooper, & Gordon*
Contemporary Speech, *HopKins & Whitaker*
Dynamics of Speech, *Myers & Herndon*
Getting Started in Public Speaking, *Prentice & Payne*
Listening by Doing, *Galvin*
Literature Alive! *Gamble & Gamble*
Person to Person, *Galvin & Book*
Public Speaking Today! *Prentice & Payne*
Speaking by Doing, *Buys, Sill, & Beck*

Theatre
Acting & Directing, *Grandstaff*
The Book of Cuttings for Acting & Directing, *Cassady*
The Book of Scenes for Acting Practice, *Cassady*
The Dynamics of Acting, *Snyder & Drumsta*
An Introduction to Modern One-Act Plays, *Cassady*
An Introduction to Theatre and Drama, *Cassady & Cassady*
Play Production Today! *Beck et al.*
Stagecraft, *Beck*

For a current catalog and information about our complete line
of language arts books, write:
National Textbook Company
a division of NTC Publishing Group
4255 West Touhy Avenue
NTC Lincolnwood (Chicago), Illinois 60646-1975 U.S.A.